How Can You Protect Yourself from Frankenstein?

Always carry a needle and thread. That way, you can offer to sew on any spare parts. Then sew his feet together.

Now you know how to save yourself from Frankenstein. But there's more to learn! Keep reading! You'll find out how to spot monsters, places to avoid, and how to monster-proof your bedroom!

HOW TO PREVENT
MONSTER ATTACKS

by DAVE ROSS

A MINSTREL™ BOOK

PUBLISHED BY
SIMON & SCHUSTER, INC.

This novel is a work of fiction. Names, characters, places and incidents are either the product of the author's imagination or are used fictitiously. Any resemblance to actual events or locales or persons, living or dead, is entirely coincidental.

A MINSTREL BOOK, published by
Simon & Schuster, Inc., 1230 Avenue
of the Americas, New York, N.Y. 10020

Published by arrangement with William Morrow and Company, Inc.
Library of Congress Catalog Card Number: 83-26536

ISBN: 0-671-63606-5

First Minstrel Books printing July, 1986

First Minstrel Books special printing August, 1986

10 9 8 7 6 5 4 3 2 1

A MINSTREL BOOK and colophon are trademarks
of Simon & Schuster, Inc.

Printed in the U.S.A.

TO MORRIS,
who kills monsters with his briefcase.

Contents

CHAPTER ONE
Monster Quiz

How many monsters can you find in this drawing?

(Answer on page 62.)

If you did not do well
on this test, you may
be in danger of a
monster attack.
Go on to Chapter Two . .

(quickly—before it's too late).

CHAPTER TWO
Monster Lineup

WANTED

FRANKENSTEIN'S MONSTER

ALIAS: Frankie

HEIGHT: 7 feet 3 inches

WEIGHT: 356 pounds

EYE COLOR: one brown, one blue

SKIN COLOR: green

DESCRIPTION: Looks like he spent too much time at the wrong end of a sewing machine.

VAMPIRES

These monsters are a real pain in the neck.

GODZILLA
MONSTERS

These monsters are not very popular
because they have a bad habit.
When traveling through town,
they tend to step on buildings and cars.

This is very depressing.

FRANKENSTEIN

Here is a monster that can keep you in stitches.

MUMMIES

Mummies are very old, very dusty,
and usually not wrapped too tightly.

GHOSTS AND POLTERGEISTS

are the unhappy spirits of dead people.

They are not much fun at parties.

Ghosts are usually pictured as white blobby shapes. For this reason they are often confused with other things.

SHEET-COVERED CHAIR

GHOST

WARNING: DO NOT SIT ON GHOST.

ALIENS

These monsters are out of this world.

SWAMP CREATURES

When fishing for swamp creatures
always bring a net—*a very big net!*

It is always open season for swamp
creatures. Unfortunately, it is usually
open season for swamp fishermen, too.

WEREWOLVES

You can expect a hairy time
with these monsters.
Especially when there is a full moon.

CHAPTER THREE

How to Spot Monsters

(before it's too late)

Be suspicious of anyone who flies
through your window dressed as a bat.
If it isn't Superman trick or treating, watch out.

Godzilla-type monsters are easy to spot.
After all, it's hard for two-hundred-foot
dragons to sneak up on anything.

You can spot Frankenstein monsters
pretty easily.
They stand out in a crowd.

(He's the one in the back
with the size-17 sneakers.)

27

Mummies can be identified by their
unusual clothing.

But they'll never win any prizes
in a best-dressed contest.

It is easy to tell if King Kong
is hiding under your bed.

Your nose will be touching the ceiling.

CHAPTER FOUR
How to Recognize a Monster Attack

(and know which monster is attacking)

If you find hands around
your throat, check them carefully.

If none of the fingers match,
it's a Frankenstein monster.

If they are bandaged,

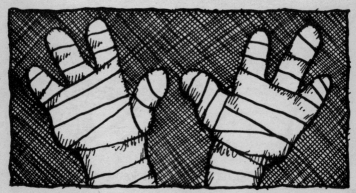

it's either a mummy or a fingernail biter.

If they are hairy and have long nails,

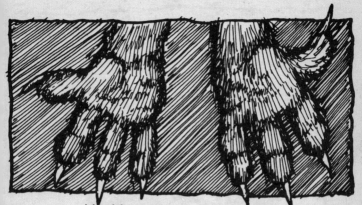

it's either a werewolf or someone
who needs a manicure really bad.

If they are slimy and have seaweed
under their fingernails,

it's a swamp creature.

If you can't see them but you know
they're there, it's a ghost.

If it is only one hand,
it's King Kong.

CHAPTER FIVE
How to Defend Against Monster Attacks

Garlic will keep most vampires away.

Unfortunately, it will keep
most friends away, too.

To stop Frankenstein-monster attacks,
carry a needle and thread.
That way you can offer to sew on any
loose parts.

(Then stitch his feet together.)

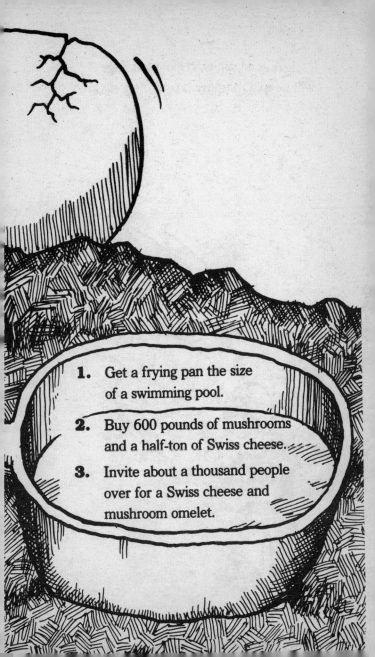

1. Get a frying pan the size of a swimming pool.

2. Buy 600 pounds of mushrooms and a half-ton of Swiss cheese.

3. Invite about a thousand people over for a Swiss cheese and mushroom omelet.

A good tug on a loose bandage
will keep a mummy busy for a long time.

If that doesn't work, give him a Band-Aid.

**While he's trying to open the wrapper,
you can get away.**

One way to avoid an alien attack
is to give it something else to attack.

Then loan it a quarter.

To protect yourself from King Kong,
buy bananas.

LOTS OF BANANAS!

CHAPTER SIX
Places to Avoid

Visits to tombs can end up being permanent.

Refrain from hitchhiking on a U.F.O.
(You never know whether you are
a passenger or the main course.)

Avoid haunted houses (especially on Halloween).

Don't scuba dive in Loch Ness.

Avoid aliens at mealtime.

CHAPTER SEVEN
How to Monster-Proof Your Bedroom

Step 1

Buy a 2000-watt night-light.

This bright idea will eliminate any shadows
a monster might hide in.

Step 2

Lock your closet door.

This will also keep your younger brothers
and sisters from messing with your clothes.

Step 3

Surround your bed with barbed wire.

Just remember to be careful when getting
up to go to the bathroom in the
middle of the night.

Step 4

Coat your bedroom floor with about
six inches of sticky peanut butter.
This will slow up most monsters.

Step 5

Wear jogging shoes to bed so you can outrun slow-moving monsters.

It's a well-known fact that monsters never attack a person completely covered with sheets.

ANSWERS TO THE MONSTER QUIZ

KEY

1. Older brother dressed as Frankenstein monster.

2. Younger sister hiding under rug.

3. Mummy in the closet.

4. Unidentified creature under bed.

5. Tarantula hanging from light.

By now you should know the correct answer is one-and-a-half monsters.

EXPLANATION:

- Only number 3 is definitely a monster attack.

- While it is true brothers and sisters act like monsters, they do not qualify for this list. Do not count 1 and 2.

- Number 4, the unidentified creature, could be a werewolf. But it's probably your pet cat. The only way to be certain is to reach under the bed. Since you are not crazy enough to do that, this only counts for one-half.

- Do not count number 5. A regular-sized tarantula (about the size of your hand) only looks like a monster. Its bite is painful but seldom fatal. Only worry about tarantulas larger than a Volkswagen.

ABOUT THE AUTHOR

DAVE ROSS has liked monsters since he was a little boy. In fact, some of his teachers remember him as a monstrous student. As an author and illustrator of children's books, Dave has over twenty-five books to his credit. His other books include *Rat Race and Other Rodent Jokes*, *A Book of Hugs*, *A Book of Kisses*, and the *Space Monster* series. Dave lives with his wife (who is not a monster) in Clifton Park, New York.